Made in the USA
Las Vegas, NV
07 June 2024

90838127R00056